## Simple Machines

# Inclined Planes

by Martha E. H. Rustad

CAPSTONE PRESS
a capstone imprint

Little Pebble is published by Capstone Press,
1710 Roe Crest Drive, North Mankato, Minnesota 56003
www.mycapstone.com



**Library of Congress Cataloging-in-Publication Data**
Names: Rustad, Martha E. H. (Martha Elizabeth Hillman), 1975– author.
Title: Inclined planes / by Martha E.H. Rustad.
Description: North Mankato, Minnesota : Capstone Press, 2018. | Series:
    Little pebble. Simple machines
Identifiers: LCCN 2017031581 (print) | LCCN 2017035879 (ebook) |
    ISBN 9781543500899 (eBook PDF) | ISBN 9781543500776 (hardcover) |
    ISBN 9781543500837 (paperback)
Subjects:  LCSH: Inclined planes—Juvenile literature.
Classification: LCC TJ147 (ebook) | LCC TJ147 .R877 2018 (print) | DDC
    621.8—dc23
LC record available at https://lccn.loc.gov/2017031581

**Editorial Credits**
Marissa Kirkman, editor; Kyle Grentz (cover) and Charmaine Whitman (interior), designers;
Jo Miller, media researcher; Katy LaVigne, production specialist

**Image Credits**
Capstone Studio: Karon Dubke, 17, 21; iStockphoto: /kali9, 11, Shinyfamily, 15; Science Source: Photo Researchers, Inc., 7; Shutterstock: BCFC, 9, Caron Badkin, 13, Grandpa, 22, Marcel Derweduwen, cover, 1, Sajee Rod, 5, wavebreakmedia, 19

**Design Elements**
Capstone

# Table of Contents

# Help with Work

Work is hard!

We need help.

Use a simple machine.

These tools help us work.

inclined plane

An inclined plane is a ramp.
We move a load up or down
the ramp.

load
ramp

# Move a Load

One end is low.

The other end is high.

A load sits at the bottom.

We move it up.

load

The load moves to the top.

It takes longer to get there.

But the work is easier.

# Everyday Tools

The train is at the bottom.

Push!

The train goes up the ramp.

A slide is an inclined plane.

Whee!

I go down fast.

Steps are an inclined plane.

Climb!

We can reach the top.

We use a simple machine.

It makes work easier and fun.

# Glossary

**inclined plane**—a simple machine that makes moving a load up or down easier; it is sloped with one end higher than the other, like a ramp

**load**—an object that you want to move or lift

**simple machine**—a tool that makes it easier to do something

**tool**—an item used to make work easier

**work**—a job that must be done

# Read More

Miller, Tim and Rebecca Sjonger. *Inclined Planes in My Makerspace.* Simple Machines in My Makerspace. New York: Crabtree Publishing, 2017.

Schuh, Mari. *Playing a Game: Inclined Plane vs. Lever.* Simple Machines to the Rescue. Minneapolis: Lerner, 2016.

Weakland, Mark. *Fred Flintstone's Adventures with Inclined Planes: A Rampin' Good Time.* Flintstones Explain Simple Machines. North Mankato, Minn.: Capstone Press, 2016.

# Internet Sites

Use FactHound to find Internet sites related to this book.

Visit www.facthound.com

Just type in 9781543500776 and go.

Check out projects, games and lots more at
**www.capstonekids.com**

# Critical Thinking Questions

1. What do we move up or down a ramp?

2. What is different about the two ends of an inclined plane?

3. What types of inclined planes have you used? How did they help you?

# Index